Kings & Monkeys

Kings & Monkeys

12 ready-to-use assemblies for primsry schools

Michael Catchpool & Pat Lunt

kevin
mayhew

First published in Great Britain in 2001 by Kevin Mayhew Ltd
Buxhall, Stowmarket, Suffolk IP14 3BW
Tel: +44 (0) 1449 737978 Fax: +44 (0) 1449 737834
E-mail: info@kevinmayhew.com

www.kevinmayhew.com

© Copyright 2001 Michael Catchpool and Pat Lunt

The right of Michael Catchpool and Pat Lunt to be identified as the authors of this
work has been asserted by them in accordance with the Copyright, Designs
and Patents Act 1988.

All rights reserved. No part of this publication may be reproduced,
stored in a retrieval system, or transmitted, in any form or by any
means, electronic, mechanical, photocopying, recording, or otherwise, without the
prior written permission of the publisher.

The publishers wish to thank all those who have given their permission to reproduce
copyright material in this publication.

Every effort has been made to trace the owners of copyright material and we hope
that no copyright has been infringed. Pardon is sought and apology made if the
contrary be the case, and a correction will be made in any reprint of this book.

ISBN 978 1 84003 742 3
Catalogue No. 1500429

Cover design by Jonathan Stroulger
Edited and typeset by Elisabeth Bates

Printed and bound in Great Britain

Contents

About the authors	6
Introduction	8
Bully-cat! Bully-dog!	9
The friendly giant	13
The proud man and his chair	17
Monkey in a waterhole	21
The sculptor's tale	27
A rather sweet story	31
The rich man and his wall	35
The old fiddler	39
The poor man and the pearl	43
The scrambled-egg chef	47
The king and the wind	53
The two farmers	57
Thematic index	61

About the authors

Michael Catchpool is a headteacher and, as a result, has done the odd assembly (very odd, some people say).

Pat Lunt, also in education, teaches in a junior school and knows a thing or two about assemblies as well (and not just the way it is spelt!).

They have collaborated on a number of projects and are the authors of *Say It – Act It!*, books 1 and 2 (another useful resource for schools) and *The Log in My Eye*, a book of double-act sketches.

Introduction

Here is a collection of stories which tell the tales of mice and giants, elephants and sculptors, kings and monkeys and many more besides. The tales are sometimes funny, sometimes poignant but always thought-provoking. The stories are intended to be used in two main ways.

First and foremost they are an original and useful resource for assemblies. Each story is accompanied by a concluding piece which explores the theme of the story and provides 'food for thought' for those moments of reflection in assembly. The theme is explored in general terms and, in addition, with a Christian emphasis, so that those leading the assembly may choose the most appropriate for their situation.

The stories are equally useful as a valuable PSHME (Personal, Social, Health and Moral Education) resource. Each story can be used as a starting point to help consider a particular issue. In addition, there is a selection of questions at the end of each story to aid or prompt discussion.

However you choose to use this book, our hope is that it is accessible, fun and a stress-free resource for the busy teacher.

Bully-cat! Bully-dog!

Story   Under a fallen tree, near a river, lived a small and very hungry mouse. On the other side of the river grew a plum tree. This was the mouse's favourite place. Every morning the mouse would scamper across the creaky bridge that went over the river and hurry to the tree. There he would nibble on the delicious plums that hung from its branches.

One morning the mouse got up, as hungry as ever, and hurried off to the bridge. But halfway across the mouse met a problem – a cat! The cat looked at the mouse and the mouse looked at the cat.

'Excuse me,' squeaked the mouse nervously, 'but I'd like to get past, so I can go over to the plum tree. Would you kindly move to one side?'

'No,' said the cat. 'I'm going to lie here in the sun and I'm not going to let you past.'

'Why ever not?' asked the mouse.

'Because I'm bigger than you, so I can do what I want, and today I am going to lie in the sun on this bridge and you cannot come over.'

The mouse looked on sadly as the cat sprawled out on the creaking planks of the bridge. It was true; the cat was certainly bigger than the mouse.

'You're nothing but a bully-cat!' squeaked the mouse angrily, but the cat just twitched her tail lazily as she lay in the warm sun. So the mouse went sadly back home.

Luckily, the mouse had a friend – a dog. And the mouse went to see him, to ask if he would help. When the dog heard all about the mouse's problem, he agreed to help at once. They whispered together and soon came up with a special plan.

Feeling much braver, the mouse made his way back to the bridge where the cat was still snoozing in the sun. 'Excuse me,' squeaked the mouse, 'but would you move, I'd like to get past!'

'Not you again!' said the cat, opening one sleepy eye slowly. 'Don't forget, I'm bigger than you; now clear off!'

The mouse looked at the cat and then he gave a squeaky sort of whistle and . . . out of the trees and onto the creaking bridge that went over the river, rushed the dog.

'And I'm bigger than you,' growled the dog to the cat, 'now out of our way!'

The cat saw that the dog was indeed bigger than she was, and she leapt to her feet and hurried off. 'You bully-dog,' she hissed as she left.

The dog and the mouse made their way over the bridge and soon the mouse was scampering up the trunk of the plum tree, nibbling on the juiciest plums he could find whilst the dog lay in the shade.

When the mouse had finished and licked his sticky paws clean, he and his friend, the dog, made their way back home.

But the cat had a friend – a nanny-goat. She went to ask if she would help and soon they came up with a special plan.

The next morning, as the mouse and the dog made their way across the bridge they found the cat lying in their way.

'Out of our way!' said the dog and the mouse together.

'No!' said the cat.

'Don't forget that I am bigger than you,' said the dog menacingly.

But the cat stayed where she was and gave a purring sort of whistle and . . . out from the trees and onto the creaking bridge that went over the river, bounded the goat.

'And I'm bigger than you,' bleated the goat to the dog and the mouse, and she showed her horns. 'Now clear off!'

The dog saw that the goat was indeed bigger than he was, and much, much bigger than the mouse, so they turned and ran.

'You bully-goat' barked the dog as they left, leaving the cat to lie out in the sun on the planks of the bridge, whilst the goat stood by chewing thoughtfully.

But the mouse had another friend – a cow. And when the mouse explained his problem the cow was keen to help. Very soon, they had come up with a special plan.

Feeling very brave indeed, the mouse and the dog made their way to the creaking bridge that went over the river. The cat was still lying there in the sun, with the goat standing silently beside her.

'Not you again,' said the cat, 'I thought we told you to clear off.'

'Yes, don't forget I'm bigger than you,' said the goat, standing with her horns pointed at the dog.

But the mouse gave a squeaky sort of whistle and . . . thundering out of the trees and onto the creaking bridge, charged the cow.

'And I'm bigger than you,' snorted the cow to the goat and the cat. 'Now clear off!'

The goat saw that the cow was indeed bigger than she was, and much, much bigger than the cat, so they quickly turned and fled.

'You bully-cow!' bleated the goat as they left.

The cow and the dog and the mouse hurried over the bridge and soon the mouse was scampering up the trunk of the plum tree and finding the juiciest plums to nibble. When he'd finally finished and washed his sticky whiskers, the mouse was so full he had to have a ride home on the cow's back.

But the cat had another friend – a horse. She told him her problem and very soon they had come up with a special plan.

The next morning, when the mouse and the dog and the cow made their way to the bridge, there, lying in the sun was the cat, with the goat standing beside her.

'Out of our way,' said the cow.

'No!' said the cat, yawning.

'Don't forget I'm bigger than you,' said the cow lowering her long horns.

But the cat just gave a purring sort of whistle and . . . rushing out of the trees and onto the creaking bridge, galloped the horse.

'And I'm bigger than you,' whinnied the horse raising his heavy hooves. 'Now clear off!'

The mouse and the dog and the cow stood on one end of the bridge; and the cat and the goat and the horse stood on the other, the two groups staring angrily at each other.

And as they stood and stared, the bridge began to creak and to groan, to sigh and to sag, until suddenly, the planks snapped and the animals tumbled over and over, down into the river below.

'Help!' squeaked the mouse as the water washed over him.

'Help!' squealed the cat as she splashed round and round.

'Help!' spluttered the dog as he began to sink.

'Help!' cried the goat as she thrashed about.

'Help!' wailed the cow as she swallowed a mouthful of water.

The horse stretched and grabbed tightly on to a branch with his strong teeth. 'Hold on!' he called and everyone did. The cow clung to the horse's tail. The goat grabbed on to the cow, the dog held on to the goat. The cat caught hold of the dog, and the mouse held firmly to the cat.

Slowly, they managed to drag themselves out of the water and lay panting on the river bank. They all looked up at what was left of the creaking bridge above them and then down at the river below.

'That river is bigger than all of us put together,' said the mouse.

'But together, we were big enough to help each other.'

And the others all agreed.

Slowly they made their way to the plum tree and there they all had so much to eat that they didn't worry about bridges or rivers, but just lay in the hot sun together, feeling very full indeed.

General theme

The way we treat each other is very important. Just because we are bigger than someone else or feel we are more powerful than them doesn't mean we can have our own way, especially if that means making someone else unhappy. In the story, the animals kept trying to stop each other doing what they wanted just because they felt like it, because they felt in a position of power. They tried to make themselves feel bigger by making others feel smaller – they were bullying each other. But in the end, they found the only way to succeed was to work together.

We all have a responsibility to be big enough and strong enough to respond to what others want and need.

That's surely a true test of just how big we are.

Christian theme

Many of the animals in the story thought they were big and powerful and could tell others just what to do. But Jesus gave a very clear example of how we should behave towards each other. Jesus had all the power of heaven and yet he didn't order people about or misuse his power. In fact Jesus said he had come to serve people, to help make their lives better.

Are we big enough to copy such a clear message about how to treat others?

PSHME ideas

This story can be used to discuss:
- Bullying
- Power
- Co-operation

- What is a bully?
- Is a bully always someone who is bigger than you are?
- If someone is unkind to you does that mean they are a bully?
- Is bullying only done by hitting other people?
- If you had a disagreement with someone, how could you begin to resolve it?
- Why do people bully?

The friendly giant

Story There was once a giant who lived on top of a hill. And at the bottom of the hill was a village. All the people in the village were scared of the giant on the top of the hill. He was huge and frightening, just as giants are. Every morning the villagers could hear him stamping about his enormous house. His feet were so large that the ground trembled every time he walked. And every night the windows of the houses in the village rattled with the giant's loud snoring.

One day the blacksmith from the village went up to the forest near the top of the hill to collect some firewood. Suddenly, he could feel the ground trembling beneath his feet. The blacksmith dropped his pile of wood and looked round in a panic. There, in the distance, he could see tall trees crashing to the floor. And as he looked, stamping his way towards him and pushing the trees away as if they were as light as grass came the enormous giant.

'Oh no,' he moaned, 'it's the giant!'

As the blacksmith nervously watched, he saw the giant pick up huge branches as if they were twigs. Soon the giant had collected an enormous pile of wood. The blacksmith stood and stared.

'Oh no,' he wailed. 'The giant is collecting wood. That means he's going to make a fire. And that means he's going to cook something. And that means we'd better look out because surely the giant is going to come down to the village, snatch some of us away and eat us for his tea! Because that's what giants do.'

The blacksmith hid behind a tree and waited for the giant to stomp his way back home. As soon as the giant was gone the blacksmith ran down to the village and told his wife all about what he had seen.

When his wife heard his story she looked terrified. 'That's terrible! We'll have to hide!' And they did – under the bed – and pulled a blanket over their heads, just in case.

Now it so happened that the miller had gone out walking with his dog. His dog ran off, up the hill towards the giant's castle.

The miller ran after his dog and when he got near the castle, being rather nosy, he peered in through one of the large windows. There he saw the giant carrying a huge saucepan towards a large fire which was burning brightly in the enormous hearth.

'Oh no,' moaned the miller, 'it's terrible. The giant has got a huge pan and a huge fire and that means he's going to cook something. And that means we'd better look out – because surely the giant is going to come down to the village, snatch some of us away and eat us for his tea! Because that's what giant's do!' And with that the miller ran down the hill with his dog following close behind and went and told his wife all that he had seen. 'That's terrible!' wailed the miller's wife. 'We'll have to hide.'

And they did – in the cupboard under the stairs. Though they did light a small candle because they were both afraid of the dark.

Now the tailor, returning from market, took a short-cut which took him by the giant's castle. And being slightly nosy, he peered in through a huge window. There he saw the giant holding an enormous knife, bigger than a soldier's sword. It glinted and flashed in the firelight as the giant carefully cut up some large vegetables.

'It's awful!' wailed the tailor. 'The giant is cutting up vegetables. That means he's going to cook something. And that means we'd better look out because surely the giant is going to come down to the village, snatch some of us away and eat us for his tea – because that's what giants do.'

The tailor turned and ran down the hill and told his wife all that he had seen.

'That's terrible!' wailed the tailor's wife. 'We'll have to hide!' And so they did – in the baby's room, behind the cot. And the tailor put a potty on his head just to be sure.

Meanwhile everyone in the village had heard about the giant's fire, the giant's saucepan and knife, and how he was going to do some cooking. And how he was coming down to the village to snatch someone away, ready to eat them, because that's what giants did. There was nothing else to do but hide. The villagers locked their doors. They bolted their doors. They put chairs . . . and tables . . . and cupboards in front of their doors. And then they hid. Some in the cellar. Some in the attic. In cupboards. In drawers. Under sheets. Behind curtains. And even in the bath. They hid and they waited. Suddenly, they felt the earth begin to tremor. And they heard their windows rattle. The giant was coming down the hill towards the village! He took huge strides and with each step the ground shook like a mini earthquake.

'He's coming! He's coming!' wailed the villagers.

The tailor cautiously lifted the potty on his head and peered out of his window. He saw the giant striding down the street, carrying his huge saucepan.

'He's coming to get us! He's coming to get us! He's going to put us in his saucepan!' said the tailor and promptly put the potty back on his head.

Suddenly there was a loud knock on the door. And then another, so heavy the door seemed as if it might break.

'W - w - w - what do you want?' stammered the tailor.

'I have come!' roared the voice of the giant.

'Y - y - y - yes?' said the tailor.

'I have come to see . . . if you'd like a drop of soup.'

'Pardon?'

'I said I've come to see if you'd like a drop of soup. You see, I've collected some wood, made a fire, got my saucepan out, cut up some vegetables and made some vegetable soup and I just wondered if any of you villagers wanted some. I've got plenty you see.'

'Oh, I see,' said the tailor, very relieved. 'Well, that is kind of you.'

'That's OK,' said the giant. 'You know, the funny thing is, there doesn't seem to be anybody around. Almost as if they were hiding.'

'Well,' laughed the tailor and his wife. 'That's because we've been a bit silly. You see, it's just that we thought . . .'

'Yes?' said the giant.

'Well, it's just that we thought . . . Oh never mind, let's have some of that soup.'

And from that day on, the villagers and the giant got on very well. And the giant often made a big saucepan of vegetable soup to share. Because that's what *this* giant just happened to do!

General theme

It's easy to look at someone and then think that you know how they're going to behave.

That's what the villagers in the story did. When they just *looked* at the giant they thought they knew how he'd behave. But it turned out they were wrong. What they needed to do was to spend some time finding out what he was really like.

All our relationships are very important and the best way to make them work is to take time to find out what people are really like.

Christian theme

In the Bible, God says, 'Man looks at the outward appearance but I look at the heart' (1 Samuel 16:7). We need to make sure that we don't judge people just on the way they look, but instead take time to find out about them so we can really get to know them properly.

PSHME ideas

This story can be used to discuss:
- Relationships
- Prejudice
- Stereotyping
- Communication

- Do you think you are good at telling what someone is like just by looking at them?
- Have you ever thought something about someone and then found out they were completely different?
- An 81-year-old lady had her handbag snatched from her in the street, just after she'd collected her pension. Three people were arrested: Dr Christopher Archer, Wayne Stevens and Miss Henrietta Hawthorne . . . who do you think snatched the bag?
- How could you go about finding out about someone whom you didn't know?
- If you had to go to a new school, how would you like the children in your new class to treat you?

The proud man and his chair

Story   There was once a rich man who was very, very proud. He believed he was the most important person in all the world. If anybody asked him to do anything he would say, 'Pah! I am too important for that!'

Now one day, the rich man decided to hold a banquet. 'This,' he said, 'is to be a magnificent banquet. The best banquet there has ever been – to show everybody just how important I am.'

So, orders were sent to the kitchens and the cooks set to work and tried their hardest to produce the most mouth-watering and tempting dishes they could think of. There were chickens roasted till they were golden brown and covered in a gravy laced with wine. There were smoked hams and smoked fish, delicately laid out on huge silver plates. There were chocolate cakes layered with fresh cream and fresh, ripe strawberries. It really was a magnificent feast.

At last it was time for the banquet to begin and one by one the guests arrived and took their place at the huge table which was covered from end to end with plate after plate and dish after dish of magnificent, mouth-watering food. The cooks had really excelled themselves. Mmmm . . . the food smelled delicious and the guests could hardly wait to begin.

The rich man was at the head of the table and was about to sit on his chair when he suddenly turned to one of his servants and said, 'No! This is not good enough!'

'What's the matter?' asked the servant a little nervously. 'Is there not enough food?'

'It's not the food, it's the chair,' said the rich man. 'The chair's not good enough!'

'Not good enough? But it's your favourite chair. You always sit on it.'

'Not any more I don't!' snapped the rich man. 'No, it's just not good enough. Not for someone as important as me. Look at it!'

'I'm looking,' said the servant, anxious to obey.

'Well, can't you see what's wrong with it?'

'Well, not really,' said the servant.

'Well, I'll tell you what the matter is,' said the rich man. 'I'm very important and this chair is too low. Look at it! It's as low as all the others. It should be higher. People who are important don't sit on low chairs. They shouldn't be low down with everybody else. It's obvious, they should be higher. Call a carpenter. Get him to make my chair higher!'

'Wouldn't you like to eat first?' said the servant, looking at all the food on the table.

'No,' said the rich man. 'I want this chair sorted out now. Call a carpenter.'

So the carpenter was called and he came to see the chair.

'My, my,' said the carpenter, looking at all the food spread out on the table, 'I wouldn't mind a bit of that myself.'

'Never you mind about the food,' said the rich man, 'I'm worried about my chair.'

'What's the matter?' asked the carpenter. 'Not soft enough for you?'

'No,' said the man, 'it's not high enough. Not high enough for someone as important as me. So I want you to make my chair higher!'

'Wouldn't you like to eat first?' said the carpenter. And all the other guests nodded, because they desperately wanted to eat first. But the rich man said, 'No! Nobody eats anything until I am happy with my chair.'

So at once the carpenter set to work making the rich man's chair higher. There was the sound of hammering and sawing as the carpenter worked. The guests hoped the carpenter would hurry up so that they could make a start on the magnificent banquet. At last he finished and the chair was certainly much higher. Slowly, the rich man climbed into his new chair, sat back and looked at everybody. He paused for a moment and then said, 'No! This is not good enough. I am a very important person so I should have a much higher chair. Carpenter, make my chair higher!'

'Should I do that after you've eaten?' said the carpenter, looking hungrily at a plump roast chicken which lay on a silver dish on the table.

'No!' shouted the rich man. 'You will do it now! Nobody eats until I am happy with my chair.'

'We were afraid of that,' muttered a few of the guests, whilst the carpenter began working on the rich man's chair. After more sounds of busy hammering and sawing, the carpenter eventually said, 'Here you are, how's this?'

The chair was certainly much higher. So high in fact that two servants had to help the rich man into the chair. There he sat and looked down at everybody. He paused for a while and then suddenly he shouted, 'No! this is not good enough!'

There was a loud groan from the guests, which the rich man ignored.

'No, it's just not good enough. Someone as important as me should have a much higher chair. Carpenter, carpenter . . .'

'It's all right,' said the carpenter, 'I think I know what's coming next. You want me to make your chair even higher.' And soon there came more sounds of hammering and sawing.

Eventually the carpenter finished and the chair was set up ready for the rich man. It was certainly much higher. So high in fact, that it took three servants and a very long ladder to actually get the rich man up into it. There he sat, perched on his chair, peering down at everybody. The rich man was now so high up that his guests and the table with the magnificent banquet all looked rather small.

Suddenly the rich man said, 'Yes! Yes, this is good. This is certainly good enough. Good enough and high enough for someone as important as me.'

The guests smiled expectantly. 'Let the banquet begin!' said the rich man grandly. The guests did just that.

'It all looks delicious,' said the rich man, sitting up on his chair, and he reached out for a piece of chicken. But he couldn't reach. He couldn't reach at all. The piece of chicken was on a plate, on the table, a long way down. And the rich man was now high up in the air on his chair. Much too high to reach any of the delicious food at the banquet. The rich man sat importantly in his lofty perch and watched as the guests ate all the delicious food. But try as he might, he couldn't reach a thing. He was just too high up. At last the banquet came to an end and the dishes were cleared away. The guests made their way home whilst the rich man still sat in his chair. Only the carpenter was left.

'Well,' he said, 'I hope you found your chair to your liking. I hope you felt important up there, looking down on everybody.'

The rich man sat quiet for a moment. 'You know, I did feel something,' he said suddenly. 'In fact I still do.'

'Oh yes,' said the carpenter, 'and what is that?'

'Hungry,' said the rich man, 'very, very hungry!'

General theme

Sometimes we can feel very important and believe we're so very special. There's nothing wrong with that. But when we start believing that we're so much more important than other people, so much better than they are and deserve better things, that's when things go wrong. That's where the rich man in the story went wrong: he began to believe he was so much better than everyone else . . . but all that happened was that he got literally further and further away from everybody. So in the end he just couldn't join in. He isolated himself and missed out.

Christian theme

In the Bible it explains that Jesus didn't isolate himself by saying he was so much better than everyone else. Instead he showed people that the way to treat others is to spend time being with them, talking with them, even serving them.

Jesus could have decided not to spend any time with other people and say he was much too important but he didn't. Instead he said that he had come to serve (Matthew 20:28). Jesus set a clear example for us to follow.

PSHME ideas

This story can be used to discuss:
- Pride
- Relationships
- Community

- Sometimes people say it is good to feel proud. Can you think of an example when it is good to be proud?
- When is pride a good thing and when is it not?
- What effect can being proud have on others?
- If you had to write a dictionary definition of someone who is a 'show-off', what would you write?

Monkey in a waterhole

Story There was once a monkey and an elephant who lived in a jungle which, when you think about it, was probably the best place for them to live.

The two of them were great friends; in fact they really admired each other. Now, you may think that it is a good thing and, I suppose, it could be. But for the elephant and the monkey it became a problem . . . a very big problem (which is not surprising when an elephant is involved).

You see, the monkey admired the elephant so much that he started saying to himself, 'Elephant is very special. You know, I wish I was like him. I mean he's so big and strong and clever. He can do lots of things that I can't. Elephant is so big that he can push a whole tree over just by leaning against it with his head. I can't do that. And Elephant is so strong that he can lift up heavy branches with his tusks; I can't do that. And Elephant is so clever that he can squirt water through his long trunk and give himself a shower. I can't do that. Oh Elephant is such a wonderful animal, I wish I could be like him!'

Meanwhile, on the other side of the jungle, the elephant was talking to himself. 'You know,' he said, 'my friend Monkey is ever so special. I wish I were like him. He can do lots of clever things that I can't. Why, he can hang upside down from a branch by his tail. I can't do that. And he is so quick and agile that he can climb to the very top of tall trees, I can't do that. And he's really clever at peeling bananas with his hands. I can't do that. Oh I wish I could be more like Monkey. It's no good being me.'

As you can see there was a problem . . . but the problem became an even bigger problem when Monkey said to himself, 'I know, I am going to try to be much more like Elephant and do the things that he does!'

Meanwhile, on the other side of the jungle, Elephant had reached a rather similar conclusion. 'I know, I shall try to be much more like Monkey,' he said.

The next morning Monkey woke up and remembered that he

was going to try to be more like Elephant because he thought Elephant was so special . . . and Elephant got up and remembered that he was going to try to be more like Monkey because Monkey was so special.

'Now then,' said Monkey, 'what is it that Elephant does? Oh yes, that's right, he pushes over trees with his head. Well, that's just what I'm going to do.' Monkey began searching for a likely tree to push over and he soon found one, not too fat or round but still pretty impressive thought Monkey. 'Now to really use my head,' he said, but no one was there to hear the joke so it was a bit of a waste.

Monkey looked carefully at the tree in front of him, then taking three deep breaths . . . and then one more just in case, he lowered his head and ran straight for the tree. Bang! Something hit Monkey very hard – very hard indeed! In fact nothing had hit Monkey; it was Monkey who had hit something . . . the tree! 'Ow, that hurt,' cried monkey as he held onto his head. 'Ow!'

Monkey slowly opened his eyes and saw that the tree was still there, exactly as it was before he had tried to push it over with his head. Monkey rubbed his head sadly. He could feel a lump begin to grow . . . ouch!

'Oh well, that didn't work. Perhaps I ought to try something else that Elephant can do. I mean, he is such a special animal and I really would like to be like him. Perhaps I could try lifting up heavy branches with my teeth.' Monkey searched around and found a suitable branch. Not too round or heavy, but an impressive looking branch just the same. After three deep breaths . . . well, four really, Monkey crouched down, opened his mouth wide and then bit onto the branch, holding it firmly with his teeth. 'Ready, steady, lift,' he said to himself (which is very difficult to say when you have a mouthful of branch). And then Monkey tried to lift. But all he managed to do was hurt his neck and end up with an unpleasant taste of bark in his mouth. The branch hadn't moved one bit. 'This is useless,' moaned Monkey, 'I'm just not as good as Elephant. Wait, I know what I can try. Elephant is able to give himself a shower by squirting water through his nose. That's what I'll try.'

So Monkey made his way down to the waterhole. He knelt by the water and after three . . . OK, four deep breaths, he stuck his nose in the water ready to suck it up and then squirt it in the air just like Elephant. But oh dear, the water just made Monkey sneeze as it went up his nose. He sneezed and he sneezed as he wandered off sadly into the jungle.

Meanwhile, on the other side of the jungle, Elephant was getting ready to try to be like Monkey. 'Now, Monkey is able to hang by his tail from a branch so that's what I'm going to try to do,' he said and went looking for a suitable branch. He found one that was not too high up and on tiptoes he was able to hang his tail over it, though he didn't seem to be able to really wrap it round the way that monkey could.

'Right, here goes,' said Elephant and he tried to hang by his tail. But all that happened was that with a loud crash, Elephant pulled the whole branch down. 'Oh dear, that's not very good!' said Elephant. 'I'm obviously not as good as Monkey; I shall have to try something else. I know, Monkey can climb to the top of a very tall tree, that's what I'll try.' So Elephant found a suitable tree. Not a really tall one, but still quite impressive.

'Right,' he said, getting himself prepared, 'I shall now climb it.' Slowly and clumsily elephant tried to lift his front feet up against the tree to start climbing, but as he leant against the tree there was a loud creaking and cracking and the tree just toppled over falling heavily to the floor.

'I'm obviously not as good as Monkey,' Elephant moaned to himself. 'I just can't do the things he can. But wait there is something else I can try. Monkey's very good at eating fruit and peeling bananas with his hands; well, that's just what I will do.' Elephant went looking and found himself a large bunch of bananas. Carefully he placed them on the floor with his trunk and then he tried peeling them with his feet.

But, oh dear, the only thing that he managed to do was squash them all completely flat.

'This is terrible,' wailed Elephant, 'I can't do any of the things that Monkey can do; he must be so much better than I am. Oh, I wish I was like him instead of like me.'

Lion, who happened to live in the jungle as well, came across the two sad animals. 'What's the matter with you?' he said to Monkey who was swinging dejectedly by his tail from a high branch and eating a banana he had just peeled.

'It's not fair,' said Monkey, 'my friend Elephant can do lots of things that I can't; he must be much better than I am. Oh, I wish I was like him.'

A little while later, Lion came across Elephant who was looking very dejected as he cooled himself off in the waterhole and gave himself a shower by squirting water through his long trunk.

'What's the matter with you?' Lion asked.

'It's not fair,' said Elephant, 'my friend Monkey can do lots of things that I can't; he must be much better than I am. Oh, I wish I was like him.'

Lion just stood there and laughed. 'I can't believe you two,' he said and he brought them together. 'Look at yourselves; don't you realise that you are both very special? Both of you have special things that you can do . . . and so both of you can be pleased that you are just who you are.'

I am pleased to say that the two friends were able to see just how silly they'd been. And, if Elephant ever wants a banana, his friend Monkey will climb a tree, pick one and peel it for him. And if Monkey ever wants a cool refreshing shower, his friend Elephant will suck up water through his long trunk and squirt it high in the air for Monkey to shower in. And you know, I'm told they're even better friends now than they ever were before.

General theme It's good to have friends and to be able to admire what they can do. But we must be careful not to forget that we are special too. We each have things that we can do well and of which we can be proud. It's these things which help to make us who we are. The animals in the story wanted to be like someone else. It took the lion to make them realise that they should be proud of who they were and what they could do.

Christian theme In the Bible it tells us how important and special each one of us is. It says that God thinks so much about us that he knew us even before we were born: 'When my bones were being formed, carefully put together in my mother's womb, when I was growing there in secret, you knew that I was there – you saw me before I was born' (Psalm 139:15). Jesus tells us that we are so important to God that he even knows the number of hairs on our head. It's good to stop and think about all the things we can do which make us unique, and to remember just how special each one of us is.

PSHME ideas This story can be used to discuss
- Friendships
- Talents
- Self-esteem

- Make a list of the things that are good about you.
- What makes you feel good about the person you are?

- How could you make others feel good about themselves?
- Is talent a natural thing, something you are born with or is it something anyone can develop?
- Where does talent come from?
- If your parents are good musicians, does that mean you will have a better chance of being good at music yourself?

The sculptor's tale

Story There was once a sculptor who was highly skilled and well respected by all. So respected in fact, that the king asked him to carve him a statue. A statue of the king himself. Of course, the sculptor was very excited and set off at once to the palace. When he arrived, the king greeted him and showed him the stone from which he was to carve the statue. And what a stone! It was a beautiful piece of brilliant white marble that glistened and shimmered and sparkled in the sunlight. The sculptor had never seen a piece of marble so wonderful. 'I certainly wouldn't mind a piece of that for myself,' he thought, 'for it is so beautiful.'

But of course, he had to begin work. And straight away he took out his chisel and his mallet and began to carve his statue of the king. Now, as he chipped away with his chisel, small pieces of the marble fell to the floor. And the more he worked, the more pieces fell to the ground. The sculptor looked down at the little white pieces and thought to himself, 'Surely it wouldn't hurt if I put one small piece of this beautiful marble into my pocket? No one will notice . . . it won't hurt.'

And so he bent down and picked up a tiny piece and put it in his pocket. And he returned to his carving, working away with his chisel and his mallet. And the more he worked, the more pieces of marble fell to the floor. The sculptor looked at them. He saw how beautifully white they were. 'Surely it wouldn't hurt,' he thought to himself, 'if I were to take just one of these small white pieces. No one will notice . . . it won't do anyone any harm.' And so he bent down and put a piece into his pocket. And then he returned to his carving. The statue of the king was really taking shape. And the more he carved, the more pieces of marble fell to the floor. And the more the sculptor looked at them and thought to himself, 'Surely it won't hurt if I take just one piece. It won't matter. It won't hurt anyone.' And so he bent down and put a piece in his pocket.

All through the morning the sculptor worked, expertly shaping the statue of the king – the head, the face, the shoulders, the arms. And all through the morning, small pieces of white marble fell to the floor. And all through the morning the sculptor would think to himself, 'Surely it won't hurt if I take just one piece. It won't matter. It won't hurt anyone.' And so he bent down and put a piece in his pocket.

By the afternoon, the statue was beginning to look very grand and the sculptor's pockets were bulging with pieces of marble. They had become so heavy that the sculptor found it hard to walk. But still he worked with his hammer and his chisel, expertly shaping the features of the king's face on the statue – the eyes, the ears, even the lines that played around the mouth of the king. And as he worked, small pieces of white marble fell to the floor. And as the sculptor saw them lying there he thought to himself, 'Surely it won't hurt if I take just one piece. It won't matter and it won't hurt anyone.' And he bent down and put a piece into his pocket.

All through the afternoon it was the same as the morning. The sculptor working on the statue and putting the pieces of white marble into his pocket. For he was sure a little piece of white marble wouldn't hurt anyone. By now, the sculptor's pockets were so full and so heavy that he could hardly move. But he carried on carving and by the evening the statue was complete. When the king saw it he was ecstatic.

'It is marvellous!' he said to the sculptor. 'A triumph! And what do you think of the piece of marble?'

'Magnificent,' replied the sculptor.

The king paid the sculptor well and returned to his palace. The sculptor packed up his chisels and his mallets and, very slowly, began to make his way home. It was a very difficult journey. The weight in his pockets meant that he could only shuffle along. Eventually he came to the wooden bridge, which led over the river and back towards his house. The sculptor shuffled on to the creaking planks and with each heavy step he took, the planks creaked and groaned even more. Suddenly there was a loud creak and crash and the planks beneath his feet split and he tumbled into the river below. The sculptor splashed and scrabbled frantically in the water, the weight in his pockets dragging him down. Luckily for him, a shepherd was walking past and seeing the sculptor struggling in the water he reached out his long shepherd's crook and shouted to the sculptor to grab onto it.

His eyes stinging and his mouth full of water, the sculptor just managed to grab hold of the wooden staff. With a huge effort, the shepherd dragged him onto the riverbank.

'Thank you,' gasped the sculptor as he slowly sat up. The shepherd looked down at him.

'What on earth happened?' he said.

'The bridge,' said the sculptor, 'it collapsed.'

'Collapsed?' replied the shepherd. 'But that bridge is strong and reliable. You must have been trying to carry something pretty heavy across it to make it break in that way.'

The sculptor looked down and shook his head sadly. He slowly reached into his pockets. 'You know,' he said, 'I thought one little white piece of marble would be fine, that it would never cause a problem. And then I thought, "What would be the problem with one or two more little white pieces?" I just never realised how they all built up so quickly and became so heavy that I could hardly move; they nearly dragged me down . . . so far I almost didn't come back up. Who'd have thought something so small could make such a difference? What a fool I have been!'

And as the shepherd helped him to his feet, the sculptor began to empty his pockets and one by one threw the pieces of marble into the water of the river. And when his pockets were completely empty, he made his way home, tired but safe.

General theme

People often say, 'Oh, it's only a little white lie. It doesn't matter.' The problem with that attitude is that we can begin to believe that it doesn't matter if we are dishonest. It is very easy for one little white lie to follow another and another as we get all too used to not being prepared to tell the truth. But dishonesty does have its consequences. We can end up hurting others by it and we can end up hurting ourselves as we become weighed down with things that aren't true. So the next time you hear somebody say, 'It's only a little white lie, it won't hurt, it doesn't matter,' just stop and think how easy it is to get into the habit of being dishonest . . . if you are not careful.

Christian theme

One of the Ten Commandments says, quite simply, 'Do not lie.' There is nothing ambiguous about this. It doesn't say, 'Do not lie, except for little white lies, because they don't matter.' It says, 'Do not lie.' Truth matters. Jesus refers to himself as the truth, 'I am the way, the truth . . .' and he also said, 'The truth will set you free'. Lies, no matter what their size, in the end will only bind us up. You may fear one lie may be discovered and so you have to tell another, and so on. And if you are not honest with people, how can you develop a relationship with them? The Bible tells us how important truth is; let's pray that we recognise this in all we say and do.

PSHME ideas

This story could be used to discuss:
- Honesty
- Relationships
- Community

- Is lying ever OK? Can you think of an occasion when you might think it would be right?
- If a friend bought a new hat and you thought it looked silly, what would you say if they asked you if you liked it?
- If someone told you a 'little white' lie, and you found out, how would you feel? Would you forgive them?
- Would you lie to get your friend out of trouble? Would it matter if it was a lie?
- How would you feel about someone who always seemed to lie?

A rather sweet story

Story There was once a man who was lucky enough to have a huge jar of sweets – his very favourite sweets. Every day he would look at the sweets in his jar. They looked so magnificent, he felt he could almost taste them. They were such wonderful colours. And when he smelt them, they smelt fantastic.

The man put the jar of sweets on his table and climbed into bed. But as he lay in bed he found it difficult to sleep. He lay there worrying. He had a terrible thought. 'What if one of my friends were to come knocking on my door and I let them into the house and they saw my jar of sweets on the table?' he thought to himself. 'Well, of course, they would want one – or even two – or maybe three! This would never do. They're such delicious sweets, I don't want to lose one of them. I know what I must do. I must put them somewhere safe . . . away from prying eyes.'

So the man got out of bed, took the jar of sweets off the table and put it on a shelf. And then he got back into bed. But he couldn't get back to sleep, because as he lay there he began to worry. 'What if one of my friends were to come knocking on my door and I were to let them in – and they looked up at that shelf and saw my jar of sweets? Well, of course they would want one – or two – or maybe three. That would never do! No, no, no! I must put them somewhere even safer.'

So, the man got out of bed, took the jar of sweets from the shelf, took a chair, stood on tiptoe on top of the chair and stretching up high, put the jar of sweets right on the top of his cupboard. And then he went back to bed.

But he couldn't sleep. Instead he just lay there worrying. 'Now what if one of my friends were to call,' he thought to himself, 'and they knocked on my door and I let them in, and they looked up and saw my jar of sweets on top of my cupboard? Well, of course they would want one, or two – or even three. And that would never do! I must put them somewhere even safer.'

So the man got out of bed, and reached up and took the jar of sweets from the top of the cupboard. Then he put the chair on top of the table, climbed up onto the table and then onto the chair and placed the jar of sweets at the very top of his tall bookshelf. And then he went back to bed. But he couldn't sleep. Instead he just lay there worrying. 'What if one of my friends were to come knocking on my door,' he thought, 'and I were to let them in and they happened to glance up and see my jar of sweets on top of my bookshelf? Well, of course they would want one, or two, or even three! And that would never do, for they are much too delicious for me to have to give any away. I will have to put them somewhere safer.'

And so the man got out of bed and hurried outside into the dark. He soon returned with the longest ladder he could find. He placed it against the trunk of a very tall tree. Then he went inside, took his jar of sweets from the top of the bookshelf and began to climb the ladder. Higher and higher he went. Step by step, rung by rung. When he peered down, it looked a long way. But he thought about his jar of sweets. He thought about any visitors who may call and he carried on climbing, higher and higher. And as he looked down again, the things on the ground seemed very small indeed. But he thought of his sweets, of how delicious they were and how he didn't want to lose any and he carried on climbing, till at last he was right at the very top. Very carefully he reached up and placed the jar of sweets onto a high branch. But as he reached, his foot suddenly slipped. He made a mad grab with his hand and managed to cling desperately to the branch, whilst the ladder toppled to the floor with a crash. Scrabbling and scrambling the man pulled himself up onto the branch where he sat, cold and forlorn, next to his jar of sweets.

It so happened that the next morning, one of his friends did come and knock at the door. They knocked and they knocked. But they got no answer. And so they turned and went away. The poor man in the tree, high up, a long way from the ground, called out, 'Help! Help!' But he was so high up his voice sounded faint and quiet. And that is why, the next day, when two more of his friends came and knocked on the door, they heard nothing. And getting no reply, they too left and went on their way.

And I'm told that if you go to the man's house and knock on the door, you'll get no reply, because he's too far up in the tree to be able to speak to anybody.

General theme Sometimes, being selfish, not wanting to share with others can actually have the effect of distancing us from our friends. It's nice when we have good things but sometimes it's good to be ready and willing to share these. And in that sharing we are able to spend time with others and strengthen the relationships we have with them.

Christian theme The Bible speaks a lot about how we like to hold on to things and how we find it difficult to share. Perhaps it's because we are afraid that we will lose out if we do. But by being ready to share we can build relationships as we talk with others and show them that they are valuable. The Bible says this is how valuable God felt people were – the most precious thing he had was his son, Jesus, and he was prepared to offer him to the world (Romans 8:32). How generous are we prepared to be as we build relationships with others rather than distance ourselves?

PSHME ideas This story could be used to discuss:
- Sharing
- Greed
- Friendship

- Which of your things do you find hard to share with other people? Why?
- Have you ever shared something with someone but then, when they had the chance, they didn't share with you? How did it make you feel?
- Imagine you had five Smarties and you could share them with two other people, which of the following ways would you choose?
  3 for one person, 2 for one person and 0 for the last person
  5 for one person and 0 for the other two
  4 for one person, 1 for one person and 0 for the last person
- How would it make you feel? How would it make them feel?

The rich man and his wall

Story There was once a rich man who decided to build himself a magnificent house. 'It is just the sort of thing I need,' he said to himself. 'People will be able to see just how rich and important I am whenever they see my magnificent house.' So the rich man called in an architect and got him to draw up some plans for his house.

The architect spent many days hard at work on the plans, and when he had finished them he showed them to the rich man.

'Hmm.' The rich man shook his head. 'I was after something grander than that. Those towers are too short, those windows too small, there are not enough columns or pillars or twiddly bits of carving. No, no, no, not grand enough. Don't forget just how rich and important I am – that's what my house should show.'

So the architect gave a sigh (though he made sure the rich man didn't hear) and off he went and drew some more plans. And when he'd finished he showed them to the rich man.

'Hmm.' The rich man shook his head. 'I was after something grander than that. These fountains aren't ornate enough, this doorway is not wide enough; the terraces are not broad enough, there's not enough turrets or spires or fancy bits of stonework. No, no, no, not grand enough, don't forget just how rich and important I am – that's what my house should show.'

So the architect gave another sigh (though he made sure the rich man didn't hear) and off he went and drew some more plans. And when he'd finished he showed them to the rich man.

'Hmm,' said the rich man, 'what wonderful towers, what a magnificent roof, what ornate pillars and what fantastic fountains. Yes, yes, yes, this is certainly grand enough for me! It will certainly show just how rich and important I am. It must be built at once.'

So the rich man called in builders to build his magnificent house. He even paid them overtime to work at weekends (well, he was very rich). And the magnificent house was built, complete with its pillars and towers and columns and terraces and fountains . . . And it really was a magnificent house.

Every day the rich man would walk up and down outside his house and admire it and think about how important it must make him look.

One day, when returning from a journey, the rich man leant out of his coach window to admire the view of his house, but to his shock and horror he couldn't see it. The trees in his garden had grown too high and were blocking the view.

'What a disaster!' cried the rich man. 'What a disaster . . . people who are travelling along this road won't be able to see my magnificent house and they won't be able to realise how rich and important I must be . . . I will definitely have to do something about that. I need *something* that people can see when they are travelling along this road.'

And he carried on his way, desperately thinking of what he could do.

Suddenly he had an idea and he called in the architect. 'I want you to draw some new designs for a magnificent wall to be built around my house and around my gardens. Not any old wall mind you, but a magnificent high wall with wonderful carvings and magnificent brickwork. Then people who are travelling along the road will see it and realise just how rich and important I am.'

The architect spent many days hard at work on the plans and when he had finished them he showed them to the rich man.

'Hmm.' The rich man shook his head. 'I was after something grander than that. The bricks are not large enough, the pattern is not bold enough, the height is not grand enough. The carvings are not ornate enough. No, no, no, not grand enough. Don't forget just how rich and important I am – that's what my wall should show.'

So the architect left and began working on some new designs. He spent many days hard at work on the plans, and when he had finished them he showed them to the rich man.

'Hmm,' said the rich man. 'The bricks are a wonderful size, the patterns are superb, the height is magnificent. Yes, yes, yes, this is certainly grand enough for me. It will certainly show just how rich and important I am. It must be built at once.'

So the rich man called in builders to build his magnificent house. He even paid them overtime to work at weekends (well, he was very rich). And the magnificent wall was built, with it's huge bricks and fancy patterns and ornate carving. And it certainly did look magnificent.

The rich man was very pleased with it.

The people in the nearby village were very impressed with it too. Whenever they passed it they would comment on how magnificent it looked.

'I'm sure a very important and rich man must live behind this magnificent wall,' they would say.

Some of them even brought their children to see the magnificent wall. 'If you work hard, my child, one day you will be able to have a wonderful wall like this,' they would say.

'You could be like this man; see how important he is, look at his magnificent wall!'

But one day the rich man fell ill. He was too ill even to get out of bed and just lay in his bed. As he fell more and more ill, he tried calling out for help. But no one heard him. Things got worse and he lay in his bed too ill and weak even to move. And though he called out for help, no one heard him and no one came.

But outside, people still gathered by the wall and looked at it admiringly. And they said to each other, 'What a rich, powerful and important man must live here, what a magnificent wall!'

General theme

The rich man's wall was certainly magnificent to look at, but the most important thing was what was behind it. And unfortunately for him, no one knew that he was lying behind it unwell and needing help. Sometimes it is hard to really get to know people because they can put all sorts of barriers in the way to stop people getting to know them. But sometimes, although someone seems big and in control and impressive, what they really need is someone to listen to them, to talk to them, to find out what they are really like. Perhaps you could spend time getting to know someone whom you haven't really talked with before, because maybe you could be just the help they need.

Christian theme

The rich man in the story had built a magnificent wall around himself. But that wall really hid what was going on in his life. He needed help and no one could see it. Jesus said, 'I have come to bring release to the captives.' This means to set people free. Although the rich man in the story wasn't in a real prison, he had shut himself in behind his wall, away from everyone else. In a way he was trapped. Some people put up a 'wall' to stop others speaking to them or finding out about them, because they are worried that they might not be liked or accepted. Jesus said he didn't want people to be like that, he wanted to release them from that fear. We can help release people by being ready to talk with them, by bothering to find out about them, and by being ready to accept them.

PSHME ideas

This story can be used to discuss:
- Expressing feelings
- Helping others
- Personal defences

- Do you sometimes find it difficult to talk about how you are feeling? Why?
- Do you think it is true, that boys and men shouldn't cry?
- What makes a good listener?
- How would you describe someone who has a 'cool' image?
- Would you ever be able to help a pop star?

The old fiddler

Story There was once an old fiddler who used to play regularly at the king's court and was a great favourite. He could play all sorts of tunes. Merry dances, tunes so sweet and mellow they would bring a tear to your eye. Jigs so lively and fast, they would not only set your feet tapping but also get you dancing. Whenever there was a special royal occasion the king would ask the fiddler to play. At banquets and feasts, at garden parties and birthdays . . . he even played at the king's wedding.

But one day, the old king fell ill. As he lay in his bed, he asked for the fiddler to play a tune for him. The fiddler played a quiet and soothing tune, which was to be the last thing the king heard.

Of course the fiddler played at the king's funeral: a sad and melancholy tune.

Now the king's son was soon crowned as the new king. 'You need a musician,' his courtiers told him. 'Someone whose music will liven up the castle.'

'What a good idea,' said the new king, 'a very good idea indeed.'

'Then,' continued the courtiers, 'why don't you invite the fiddler back to the castle? The late king, your father, enjoyed his music so much, as did we all. He could play such wonderful tunes.'

But the new king sat and thought for a moment. 'You know,' he said, 'I think I've had enough of listening to the sound of fiddles; I much prefer a different musical instrument. Something more regal, you know, like a trumpet. Yes, yes, that's it . . . a trumpet. Find me someone who can play a trumpet . . . and play it well; and tonight we shall have a banquet and the new trumpeter will provide the music.'

So the courtiers went out to find a trumpeter to play at the new king's banquet.

When the fiddler heard there was to be a banquet, he was very excited. 'A banquet,' he said to himself. 'No doubt I'll be asked to play some tunes for the new king and to lead the music for the dances.'

And he hurried to the castle. But when he got there, the guards asked him what business he had.

'Well,' explained the fiddler, 'if there is to be a banquet tonight, then surely the king will want me to play.'

'I'm afraid not, for the new king has decided he would like to hear a trumpeter playing at the banquet. And so a trumpeter it will be.'

The fiddler could hardly believe his ears. 'The new king wants to hear a trumpeter and not the fiddler. Is that really true?'

'Indeed it is,' said the guards.

The fiddler turned his back and began to walk off, but the guards called after him. 'Wait a minute, we have all heard your wonderful music, why don't you play a tune for us?'

The fiddler turned and scowled at them. 'Play a tune for you?! Let me tell you, I have played music for the king and at the king's own request. Do you think I would bother to play my fiddle for the likes of you? You're just common soldiers. No, my music is for a king and if a king won't hear it, then no one shall,' and off he went.

The fiddler made his way home through the village. As he made his way through, he was greeted by several people. They were all excited to see him. 'Have you heard?' they said. 'The new king is going to have a great banquet tonight. I expect you've been asked to play, what dances will you be playing?'

The fiddler turned on them with a scowl. 'I have *not* been asked to play at the banquet, apparently the new king prefers the sound of a trumpet.'

'That is a shame,' said the villagers. 'But we all enjoy your magnificent music. Won't you play a tune for us?'

'Play a tune for you?! Let me tell you, I have played music for the king and at the king's own request. Do you think I would bother to play my fiddle for the likes of you? No, my music is for a king and if a king won't hear it, then no one shall,' and off he went.

At last, the fiddler returned home. His wife and family were very excited. 'Have you heard the news? The new king is going to hold a banquet. No doubt you'll be asked to play your fiddle for the dances.'

'No, I have *not* been asked to play at the banquet, apparently the new king prefers the sound of a trumpet.'

'Oh, well, never mind,' said his family. 'We all know how wonderful your music is, why don't you play a tune for us?'

'Play a tune for you?! Let me tell you, I have played music for the king and at the king's own request. No, my music is for a king and if a king won't hear it, then no one shall,' and the fiddler stormed off and locked his fiddle away in an old chest which he kept under his bed.

And no matter how often his family and his friends begged him to play them a tune, he refused and said that his music was for a king.

Now it just so happened that after a while the king became rather bored of the sound of the trumpet.

'It's too loud,' he told the courtiers, 'too brash, I want something lighter and more jolly. What do you suggest?'

'Well,' the courtiers said, 'do you remember the fiddler whose music your father so enjoyed, tunes so lively and fun they would put a smile on the sternest face and set everyone dancing?'

'The very thing,' said the king, 'fetch me the fiddler at once!'

The fiddler was sent for and asked if he would play his fiddle for the king. The fiddler felt so proud and excited. He hurriedly dragged the old chest from under his bed, unlocked it and took out his fiddle. Then he rushed up to the castle.

The fiddler stood in front of the king and bowed. 'Your majesty, it is my honour to play for you.' And he began to play.

But oh dear! The fiddle had been lying in the chest, under the bed, for so long, and since the fiddler had not bothered to practise in all that time, he could hardly play. The fiddle screeched and squealed as the fiddler tried to play.

'Stop, stop!' the king ordered. 'That's enough, in fact, that's more than enough. Take him away and his awful music . . . and bring back my trumpeter at once; at least he plays music fit for a king.'

And so the trumpeter was sent for whilst the old fiddler made his way sadly back home.

General theme

The fiddler was only prepared to offer the talent he had to the person who he thought was important – the king. Although his family would have enjoyed listening to his music, he was not prepared to share it with them. It was a pity that they were not able to enjoy his talent and that he was not prepared to share it with them. And in the end, everyone missed out.

We can sometimes be guilty of only being prepared to do things if there are people we want to impress. Just like exercise, the longer you go without doing something, the harder it is when you do try to do it. Don't leave it too long before you are prepared to do something for others.

Christian theme

Jesus often talked about the Pharisees and their attitude towards others. Sometimes, he said, they did things just for show. They were concerned just with what important people would think of them. But Jesus said we shouldn't be like that. The fiddler in the story was only concerned about impressing the king, not about sharing his talents with others. Are we the sort of people who are prepared to share with others, or will we just let what we can do go unused and wasted?

PSHME ideas

This story can be used to discuss:
- Abilities
- Sharing
- Talents
- Motivation

- What talent are you most proud of?
- What one thing would you like to be really good at? Why?
- If you were the top scorer in your school's football/netball team, how would you feel if you were only picked as substitute for the next match?
- Why might someone decide to become a pianist/concert pianist?

The poor man and the pearl

Story There was once a poor man who set off to the sea to fish. He took with him his fishing rod, a net and a basket for any fish that he caught. For the whole morning the poor man cast his line into the sea, but he only caught a few fish. Each one he put into his basket. 'This is not good, not good at all,' said the poor man. 'I've hardly caught a thing. Perhaps I should try fishing with my net instead of my rod.' So the poor man put his fishing rod down and picked up his net. Carefully he prepared himself, and after a count of three he threw the net out into the deep sea. The poor man waited on the beach, sitting in the hot sun, whilst he hoped his net would fill with fish. 'Just think,' he said to himself, 'if my net was full of fine fish I would be able to take them to the market and sell them all for a good price. Of course, I'd keep the very best one for myself and I could cook it for my tea. Oh, I hope my net is bursting with fine, silver fish.' And with that the poor man began to pull in his net. As he pulled the net in, he began to frown. He hardly had to struggle or strain as he pulled on the rope. 'Oh dear,' he thought, 'my net feels light, far too light; there can't be many fish in here.'

And by the time he had hauled the whole net onto the sand, he realised he was right. In fact there were no fish in his net at all, just one white shell with a few strands of slimy, green seaweed hanging from it.

'I can't believe it,' said the poor man. 'I've tried with my fishing rod and had no luck, and now I've tried with my net and all I've caught is this one old oyster shell. What a waste.'

The poor man carefully untangled the oyster shell from the net. 'Oh well, at least it is something to eat before I try again.' And with his knife he prised open the shell.

But when he peered inside the man could not believe his eyes. There, lying nestled inside the shell, was the most beautiful pearl the poor man had ever seen. It was as creamy white as milk and as smooth and round and perfect as a full moon. And what a size it was. The poor man had never seen a pearl as large.

Still hardly able to believe it, the poor man carefully removed the pearl and put it safely in his pocket. And then, gathering up his net and his rod, he hurried back home.

As soon as he was home the poor man hurried round to his friend's house to show him the magnificent pearl.

'It is amazing,' his friend said. 'I've never seen such a magnificent pearl; it is so beautiful, you are so lucky.'

'I know,' the poor man smiled, carefully replacing the pearl in his pocket.

From that day on, the poor man would spend each evening looking at his pearl. He would place it on a piece of cloth, laid carefully on the table, and stare at it.

One evening, as he looked at the pearl, the poor man thought to himself, 'You know, I have heard about lots of different jewels in the world with magnificent bright colours. There are emeralds that shine a brilliant green; there are rubies that are as red as summer roses and sapphires that are as blue as the sky, but my pearl is just white . . . plain and boring white. I really ought to do something about it. I can't really call it a proper jewel when there are so many other more colourful ones around.' And right there and then, the poor man searched in his cupboards and found an old tin of purple paint and a brush. Carefully he began to paint his white pearl, until it was completely covered in bright purple paint.

'Now that looks more like a proper jewel,' he said to himself. 'That's just like all those other colourful jewels I've heard about.'

The next day, when the poor man showed his purple pearl to his friends they were rather shocked.

'What have you done?' they said. 'What's happened to your beautiful white pearl?'

'It wasn't beautiful,' said the poor man. 'It was dull and boring, but now look at it! It is like all those other colourful jewels; isn't it magnificent?'

But his friends just shook their heads.

Each evening the poor man would proudly place his purple pearl on a cloth on the table and gaze at it, until one evening he thought to himself, 'You know, there are so many jewels in the world that are a much more interesting shape than mine. Just think about the way that a diamond looks . . . all those cleanly cut facets that catch the sunlight and make it sparkle like a mountain stream. But my pearl is just round. What I need to do is change the shape of my pearl.' And without wasting another moment the poor man searched in his cupboard and found a large chisel and a mallet. 'Now I will make my pearl into a much more interesting shape.' Carefully he put the chisel against the purple pearl . . . with a huge swipe of the mallet the pearl was shattered into a million tiny pieces that scattered across the floor and disappeared down the cracks in the floorboards – every single piece!

General theme

The poor man in our story just couldn't appreciate the wonderful thing he had – the beautiful pearl. He just wasn't satisfied; he'd convinced himself that the other jewels were better, and in the end he only succeeded in ruining what he had. Sometimes we can be so concerned with what other people have or other things we've seen, that we miss what we actually have. We might hear other people talking about things, or even see adverts telling us just how good certain things are, and then we get obsessed about having them. Sometimes we need just to stop and think about the wonderful things we do have and really appreciate them. Surely that's a much better feeling than being dissatisfied all the time?

Christian theme

The poor man in the story just wasn't satisfied. He had found a wonderful pearl but he wanted to change it, to make it into something different, to be like something else he'd seen. What a pity that he ended up ruining something so beautiful. In Philippians 4:11-13, Paul says, 'I have learnt to be content with all things.' Can we be content with what we have, rather than always wanting more or something different? Can we appreciate some of the wonderful things we actually do have?

PSHME ideas

This story can be used to discuss:
- Contentment
- Possessions

- Can you think of any really precious things that you have? Would you change them?
- Some people change their car for a new one every year. Why do you think they do that?
- What things make you happy or content?
- What would stop you from feeling happy or content?

- Have you ever seen something on an advert and then gone out and bought it, or asked someone to get it for you, perhaps for Christmas or a birthday?
- What made you want it – why did you feel you needed it?

The scrambled-egg chef

Story

There was once a young man named Guy, who dreamed of being a chef for a famous noble or a rich lord. His dreams began one day when he made scrambled eggs on toast for his mother and father.

'Why, these are the best scrambled eggs on toast I have ever tasted!' declared his father.

'Absolutely delicious,' agreed his mother.

And that was that. From that day on, whenever the family felt like eating scrambled eggs, it was Guy's job to prepare it.

Guy grew up and soon it was time for him to leave home and find himself a job. As luck would have it, he found a nobleman who was after a chef, so, of course, Guy applied for the job.

'Before I employ you,' said the nobleman, 'you must prepare a meal for me. Nothing too fancy though, for I do not feel terribly well today.'

'Perhaps some scrambled eggs?' suggested Guy.

'An excellent idea,' smiled the nobleman and nodded as Guy left to begin preparing the food.

In a short while Guy returned and placed the scrambled eggs before the nobleman.

'Good colour,' said the nobleman enthusiastically. He picked up his knife and fork and cut through the eggs. 'Good texture,' he went on. He cut a small piece and, as Guy nervously watched him, popped it into his mouth. He closed his eyes. He chewed. He smiled. 'Mmmm,' he said, 'good taste too! Indeed, these are probably the best scrambled eggs on toast that I have ever tasted!'

'Thank you, sir,' said Guy.

'You can start work in my kitchens straight away,' continued the nobleman, 'and every time I want scrambled eggs on toast, I want you to make it for me.'

'Yes, sir. Thank you, sir,' said Guy, bowing as he left the room.

And so Guy became a chef in the kitchen of a great nobleman, just as he had dreamed for so long, working alongside all the other chefs who had their many duties to perform. And each and every day, the nobleman would ask for scrambled eggs on toast for his breakfast. And each and every day the message would come back to the kitchen that he had found the scrambled eggs to be the best he had ever tasted. And so life went on for a time, with Guy happily making scrambled eggs on toast and the nobleman happily eating it.

Then came the day when it was announced that the nobleman was to host a huge banquet for some very special people. The other chefs in the kitchen were very excited.

'A banquet!' declared one of them. 'What an opportunity to show off our talents.'

'Oh yes!' agreed another. 'I will make a starter for the banquet. A mousse, I think. A seafood mousse.'

The other chefs gathered round as the starter was described. 'A seafood mousse of crabmeat, smoked haddock and plaice, delicately flavoured with fresh garden herbs and a hint of lemon. This will be a starter to remember!' And the other chefs agreed that it certainly would be.

Now, as Guy stood there listening to the plans for the delicious starter, he thought to himself, 'Perhaps I could make a starter for the banquet. A . . . um . . . a soup perhaps. A soup made with fresh vegetables. Yes, that's it! A soup made with fresh vegetables all lightly softened in butter and simmered gently in some stock and seasoned with herbs and spices to add a touch of the exotic. Yes, that would do!'

Then Guy began to worry. 'But what if I leave the vegetables in the butter for too long and they burn, or the stock I make is too strong, or I put too much spicy seasoning in and the whole thing is ruined? Oh no! There are just too many things that could go wrong. I don't think I will make a soup for the banquet after all.'

While he stood worrying, another chef began to imagine the marvellous main course he would prepare. 'Pheasant, I think,' he said. 'Pheasant rubbed with garlic and marinated in the juice of juniper berries, then filled with lemon and tarragon and roasted until golden brown and succulent.'

Guy listened carefully and thought to himself, 'I could make a main course for the banquet. A joint of beef, perhaps, boned and rolled around a superb stuffing of onions and herbs, served with a sauce made of the finest wine. Yes, that would do!'

But then Guy began to worry. 'But what if the joint of beef unrolled during the cooking and all the stuffing fell out? Or what if the wine sauce became sour with cooking and the whole thing was ruined? Oh no! There are just too many things that could go wrong. I don't think I will make a main course for the banquet after all.'

While he stood worrying another chef began to imagine the marvellous dessert he would prepare. 'A delicious concoction of meringues, strawberries and whipped cream,' he began. 'Egg whites beaten with sugar, and baked slowly until they are golden brown on the outside and pure white and moist inside. Added to these meringues, a mixture of strawberries soaked in peach wine and blended with fresh whipped cream. Oh yes, this will be a dessert to remember!'

Guy listened carefully and then he thought to himself, 'I could make a dessert for the banquet. An orange-chocolate soufflé perhaps. Egg yolks, flour, milk and sugar blended together. The juice and grated rind of oranges mixed with melted chocolate. All baked in the oven until the soufflé is risen, and then dusted with icing sugar and served with a garnish of orange slices. Yes, that would do!'

But then Guy began to worry. 'But what if the soufflé did not cook in the centre and it was all runny and gooey, or it was overdone and the mixture dried out and it was like eating burnt biscuits, or the whole thing collapsed as soon as it came out of the oven and was ruined? Oh no! There are just too many things that could go wrong. I don't think I will make a dessert for the banquet after all.'

And so the time of the great banquet came and the chefs in the kitchen worked feverishly in preparation, boiling, beating, mixing, melting, stirring and seasoning. And the aromas of their cooking filled the great nobleman's house.

And up in his room, Guy could smell the delicious food too. From his window he could see the guests arrive for the banquet and soon he heard the cheers and roars of approval as each magnificent course was served – the starter, the main course and the dessert.

'Ah yes,' Guy said to himself, 'maybe those cheers could have been for me, but what if it had all gone wrong? That would have been a disaster! No, the risk was just too much. I will stick to what I know I can do. I will just make scrambled egg.'

And that is exactly what he did – made scrambled egg, day after day after day!

General theme

Life is full of risks. Some of them can put us in real danger and are definitely not worth taking. But sometimes we are faced with a chance to try something new – to try new skills or perhaps develop ones we already have. These sorts of risks can be well worth taking, as they give us a chance to grow and develop.

Poor Guy in the story was too scared to take a risk – to try to develop his skills as a chef. He was too worried it would all go wrong. And in worrying, he ended up doing nothing.

Are we ready to develop the skills we have by being prepared to try? Or are we so worried we might fail, we do nothing at all?

Christian theme

We can be faced with risks every day and some of these should be avoided if possible – we don't run across a busy road or jump into a fast flowing river. But there are other risky things in life we may come across. Trying new things can seem risky: joining a new club, starting a new school, even making new friends. Even though these things may seem risky or make us nervous, the Bible tells us how God has told us not to be afraid because he is there.

That knowledge could help us when we are faced with new challenges.

PSHME ideas

This story could be used to discuss:
- Risks
- Relationships
- Dealing with hurt
- Dealing with failure
- Developing character

- Which do you think would be most scary to do – abseiling, parachute jumping, bungee jumping?
- What's the most risky thing you have ever done?
- Does something that is risky have to be something that could put you in physical danger?
- Some people say that making new friends can be a challenge. What do you think they mean?
- There is an old proverb that says, 'Better to have tried and failed than never to have tried at all.' Why do you think people might say that?
- What things do you think might be challenging when you go to Secondary School?

- How do you feel when you are faced with a new challenge?
- How do you cope when you have to try something new?
- Can you think of a time when you were faced with something new and you chose not to try it and then you wished you had?
- Can you think of a time when you were faced with something new and you tried it? How did you feel?

The king and the wind

Story There was once a king – a very proud king. And although he was proud, all his courtiers (the attendants in the court) thought the king was magnificent and longed to be near him.

One day, the king decided he would go out for a short walk. On hearing this, there was great excitement in the court and, of course, everyone wanted to go with him.

At once, the courtiers hurried off to their rooms to change into their finest clothes, to accompany the king on his walk.

At last, they were ready and they all set off. The king had one servant to carry his crown in case it got too heavy on his head as he walked along. Another carried a large umbrella to shade the king from the sun if it got too strong. Another carried a spare pair of shoes in case the ones the king was wearing got too uncomfortable. Still more servants carried spare pairs of socks in case the king fancied a change. And of course, that's not to mention the servants whose job it was to carry the five different types of drinks in case the king got thirsty, and those who carried the royal picnic hamper in case the king got hungry, and the one who carried the royal hankie in case the king sneezed. What a procession!

Of course, the courtiers thought it was magnificent and were so pleased to be involved. They marched along happily beside the king, declaring what a wonderful and noble king he was. And because the king enjoyed hearing them say such things, he happily got them to repeat it. Which, of course, the courtiers were very pleased to do, which only made the king feel even more proud.

Perhaps it was hearing all those wonderful things said by the courtiers, or perhaps it was just because he was a very vain and proud king anyway, that the king suddenly stopped and called out in a loud voice, 'I want you all to listen to me.'

The servants and the courtiers gathered round so that they could hear clearly.

'Since I am such a magnificent king, it is not right that I should have to walk with the wind blowing in my face, where it

53

can ruffle my hair or even blow things into my eyes. Instead, I have decided that from this moment on I will only walk with the wind at my back. That way it will help me along as I walk.'

Immediately, there was a burst of applause and cheering from the courtiers and servants.

'What a very sensible decision to make,' they said. 'We always knew you were a magnificent king and this just goes to show how magnificent you are. Of course you should not have to walk with the wind blowing in your face, ruffling your hair or even blowing things into your eyes. It is only right that a king as magnificent as you are should only walk with the wind at his back.'

So one servant was ordered to find out which direction the wind was blowing, and after much licking of fingers and holding them up in the air, he finally decided that the wind was blowing from the east. Then the king and the servants and the courtiers all turned round and set off in the opposite direction so that the king could have the wind blowing at his back.

The procession marched on, looking very splendid indeed. All was going well, until the wind suddenly changed direction. It was now no longer blowing from the east, but from the west.

'Stop!' the king ordered. 'I must have the wind at my back.'

So the king, the servants and all the courtiers turned round and set off in the opposite direction so that the king could walk with the wind at his back.

'What a marvellous king,' the courtiers said, 'how lucky we are to have a king who is so special that he only walks with the wind blowing at his back.'

On they went, until the wind suddenly changed direction. This time it was blowing from the south. So the king and the servants and the courtiers turned round and set off in the opposite direction so that the king could walk with the wind at his back.

On and on they walked, and every time, just when it seemed they might be getting back to the castle, the wind would change direction, the king would shout, 'Stop!' and everyone would have to turn round and set off in the opposite direction so the king could walk with the wind blowing at his back.

On and on they marched, twisting and turning with every change of the direction of the wind.

They never did get back to the castle, and I'm told if you go out looking, you'll still find them walking and changing direction whenever the wind changes, because the king is so proud, he will only walk with the wind at his back.

And all the courtiers and servants are still following wherever he goes.

General theme

Sometimes certain people might seem very popular. You might be impressed by the things they do and want to be seen to be with them and do the things they do. The courtiers in the story were very impressed with the king and wanted to be associated with him no matter what. But what a pity the poor courtiers weren't sensible or courageous enough to stop and realise the king was someone whom it was rather silly to follow. They would certainly have got home a lot sooner had they realised.

We need to take time to really think about whom we want to follow or copy. Are we following them because we agree with them or are we just doing it because others are and we don't want to feel left out? It is important to make up our own minds whether someone who seems popular is actually doing the right thing. Can we manage that today?

Christian theme

There is a story in the Old Testament about three friends called Shadrach, Meshach and Abednego (Daniel 3) who were prepared to stop and think about whom they would follow. There was a powerful king who everyone else wanted to associate with, to be seen to be doing the same things as him. But one thing he wanted everyone to do was to bow down and worship a golden statue. Shadrach, Meshach and Abednego weren't prepared to do that; they were only prepared to worship God. Although the king was popular and people were keen to follow him, Shadrach, Meshach and Abednego couldn't and wouldn't agree to. They knew the right thing to do and they had the courage to carry it out. We all need the courage to make up our own minds whether someone who seems popular is actually doing or saying the right thing. Can we manage that today?

PSHME ideas

This story can be used to discuss:
- Peer pressure
- Decision-making
- Relationships
- Popularity

- What makes someone popular?
- Which famous person is a good role model?
- Would you be prepared to be seen as different from others in your class?

- If ten of you didn't agree with something that *one* person was saying or doing, what would you do?
- If *you* didn't agree with what ten people were saying or doing, what would you do?

The two farmers

Story There were once two farmers whom we shall call Ted and Tom, for the simple reason that those were their names.

Ted and Tom lived next door to each other. They were farming neighbours.

Ted was a well-respected farmer who worked for the king. He was in charge of the king's stables and what Ted didn't know about horses just wasn't worth knowing. He could spot a good horse from a mile away. (Well, obviously not quite that far because his eyesight wasn't that good, but he knew a good horse when he saw it.) He could tell if a horse was ill or even about to become ill, just by the way that it trotted in the morning.

Ted was the best stable manager the king had ever had.

Tom was not. Tom did not work at the king's stables; in fact, he didn't work for the king at all. He just worked on his own little farm, keeping himself busy day by day.

Now, it just so happened that Ted and Tom both acquired a new animal on exactly the same day.

Tom looked at his animal and thought to himself, 'If I am to look after my animal really well, then what I need is a bit of advice, a little bit of help. And I can think of no one better for advice than my neighbour Ted, he knows everything. Just look at the magnificent animals he is in charge of down at the king's stables. Every one of them is magnificent; people are always commenting on how wonderful they are. So if anyone knows what I should do, Ted is the man. Why, he even got a new animal on exactly the same day I did.'

Tom set off to go and ask his neighbour for some help and advice. But as he walked across to Ted's farm, Tom began to have a few doubts. 'Hang on,' he said to himself, 'if I go over to Ted and ask for advice on how to look after my new animal, it will look as if I don't know what I'm doing; it will make me look stupid.'

Tom stood and leant against the wall that ran between his farm and Ted's. 'Yes, if I go asking for help, Ted will think I can't do my job properly; he'll probably laugh in my face. No, no, no, I can't have that. I shall have to think of something else instead.'

Tom stood there, thinking carefully about what he could do. 'Aha,' he said suddenly. 'All I need to do is keep a careful watch and see what he does for his new animal, and I shall do the same. I won't have to ask him a thing and I won't end up looking silly.'

So that very evening, Tom crept along in the dark, until he came to the wall between Ted's farm and his own. He peered over and watched what Ted was doing – the way he groomed and fed and looked after his animal – and then Tom tiptoed back and did exactly the same.

Each day it was the same. Tom would creep along to the wall and peer over. Secretly, he would watch Ted and then he would creep back again and try exactly the same things.

'My, my, my,' said Tom one evening as he peered over at Ted's. 'That animal of his is magnificent; it looks so fine and healthy and noble. I must be doing something wrong as mine looks decidedly ill. I must watch more carefully, perhaps I'm missing something.'

But although he watched very carefully indeed, there didn't seem to be anything he'd missed. (Of course, if he had missed it he wouldn't have known that he'd missed it, or otherwise he *wouldn't* have missed it, but I'm sure you get the point).

The weeks went by, and although his animal was not looking quite as well as he had hoped, he consoled himself with the fact that he was doing exactly the same as Ted, so that must be right.

A few days later it was announced that there was going to be a grand parade and anyone who wanted to could ride in it.

There was great excitement as people discussed the honour of riding in the parade, of what they'd wear and how they would try to look their best.

Although Ted worked for the king and was used to parades and processions, the chance to ride in one himself was very appealing so he set to work preparing his animal for the big day. He brushed and groomed with expert hands and then carefully plaited the tail and mane with brightly coloured ribbons. His animal looked magnificent.

And all the time, Tom was watching very carefully as he peered over the wall. As soon as Ted was finished, Tom hurried home and tried to do all the things he'd watched Ted do.

The day of the parade arrived. All round the village people tightened saddles and stirrups as they prepared to ride in the parade.

The streets were lined with people as the parade began. As each person passed by, a great cheer went up. In came Ted and Tom riding their new animals and both looking very pleased. As Ted rode by a huge cheer echoed along the street.

'What a magnificent animal!' people called out. 'Have you ever seen such a magnificent horse?'

But as Tom rode by on his new animal, there was no cheering, just loud laughter and shouts or derision.

'Look at him!' they shouted. 'Look at him, have you ever seen anything so stupid?'

'What's the matter with you,' Tom shouted back at the crowd. 'I have looked after my animal just as well as Ted. I have groomed it and fed it just the same. Look, it even has plaits and ribbons the very same colour. So why are you cheering him and not me? Aren't both our animals magnificent?'

'Oh yes,' the crowd laughed, 'but he is riding a magnificent horse. You are riding a magnificent cow.'

General theme

Tom, the farmer in the story who owned the cow, didn't stop and think for himself at all. He just happily copied his neighbour, whether it was the right thing to do or not. It's no surprise everyone laughed at him when he came riding into town. We too need to be prepared to stop and think for ourselves, to make sure that what we are doing is right – right for us and the circumstances and situation we are in – and not just copy others because it seems like an easy option.

Christian theme

It is sometimes easier not to have to think for yourself, but just to copy what others say and do, just like the farmer in the story. However, as he found out, it is not necessarily the best way to go about things.

Jesus questioned that way of thinking and he challenged the disciples to think for themselves. On one occasion he first asked them, 'Who do people say I am?' The disciples were quick to say what other people thought: 'Some say you are John the Baptist, others say Elijah or others say Jeremiah or some other prophet' (Matthew 16:15). But Jesus went further by asking them, 'Who do *you* say I am?' He was encouraging them to be the sort of people who were ready to think for themselves, to make their own decisions. Can we be the sort of people who can do that?

PSHME ideas

This story can be used to discuss:
- Individuality
- Decision-making
- Thinking for yourself

- How do you feel if someone copies your work or your ideas?
- Why do you think some people copy other people's work or ideas?
- Have you ever been tempted to copy someone else's work? Did you do it, or not? What stopped you?
- There is a saying that 'imitation is the sincerest form of flattery.' What do you think that means?
- Whose opinions do you trust the most? Are they always right?
- What do you think the phrase 'speak your own mind', means?
- Can you think of an occasion when you had to 'speak your own mind'?

Thematic index

Abilities	The old fiddler
Bullying	Bully-cat! Bully-dog!
Communication	The friendly giant
Community	The proud man and his chair
	The sculptor's tale
Contentment	The poor man and the pearl
Co-operation	Bully-cat! Bully-dog!
Decision-making	The king and the wind
	The two farmers
Developing character	The scrambled-egg chef
Expressing feelings	The rich man and his wall
Failure	The scrambled-egg chef
Friendship	Monkey in a waterhole
	A rather sweet story
Greed	A rather sweet story
Helping others	The rich man and his wall
Honesty	The sculptor's tale
Hurt	The scrambled-egg chef
Individuality	The two farmers
Motivation	The old fiddler
Peer pressure	The king and the wind

Personal defences	The rich man and his wall
Popularity	The king and the wind
Possessions	The poor man and the pearl
Power	Bully-cat! Bully-dog!
Prejudice	The friendly giant
Pride	The proud man and his chair The rich man and his wall
Relationships	The proud man and his chair The scrambled-egg chef The sculptor's tale The king and the wind The friendly giant
Risks	The scrambled-egg chef
Self-esteem	Monkey in a waterhole
Sharing	A rather sweet story The old fiddler
Stereotyping	The friendly giant
Talents	Monkey in a waterhole The old fiddler The scrambled-egg chef
Thinking for yourself	The two farmers